The
First
Letter

emma clark

emma clark

Contents

emma clark

Introduction:

When you close your eyes, and you're flashed with memories.
Your first times, first loves, first heartaches, and anything that
has created you into who you are and who you will slowly become.
This wasn't something I just sat and wrote from start to finish.
This was throughout all of my firsts, growing up, and falling in
and out of love. This has been a part of my life, and now I can share.
I hope you love this as much as I have loved putting it together.
This is the book to pick up when you question it all.
Thank you for reading.

All of the love,

Emma Clark

emma clark

emma clark

Winter

I wanted love
You wanted lust
We craved two different things
Until you decided it wasn't good enough for you

Anymore
-your goodbye will forever be the one that hurt the most

emma clark

What happened to forever?
You promised you would never hurt me
Yet that is exactly what you did
You broke me in ways I didn't even know I could bend

Why does it hurt so much?
Why can't two people destined to be in love just get the
"happy ever after"?
Why couldn't you just stay instead of leaving me all alone?
Having to start over
And that thought…
Of loving someone new
Makes me *nauseous*

There was a girl
She loved a boy with every piece of her heart
She gave all she could until she couldn't anymore

One day,
After all of the time they spent together,
He spoke the words no one ever wants to be told...
"This isn't what I want anymore"

See,
Here is the thing
You can't just stop wanting someone you spent so long loving
You can't just choose to walk away

Love doesn't work that way

And if in some mysterious way you can

He never loved her

You can't express to two people to love the same way

Everyone does it different

It doesn't mean running away is an expression

emma clark

You may understand
You may never will
I wanted you to crave me the way I craved you
I wanted your hands gripping my entire body
Rushing every bit of adrenaline our souls make

I have been hurt so much before that in a sick way
I never expect people to stay
I just want someone to feel consumed by me
I want to be someone's home

I'd like to believe we were meant for each other...
We just didn't do it right

I want you to show me you care about me
without gliding your hands down
my body

*I **missed** you*

You always put too much creamer in your coffee
Because you hated the taste
You kept wearing your same tight clothes
Just to prove you were bigger than before

When you were happy,
You would make that weird cackling laugh
You said my jokes were dumb, only because you never
wanted to admit that I might've actually been funnier than you
I noticed all of the little things
The way you put your clothes on
To the way you took them off

I payed attention to everything you did because you were
everything to me

That's the problem with love in today's world,
You mainly have one person who fights, chooses, and sacrifices
everything just so the other will…

Stay

I know you love him but it is time to be over

You loved with your heart and fought with your entire being

Until you were consumed

It was almost like being taken away from every decision

You were blinded
If you could've just looked through the window instead of the rearview

You could've been done a long time before now

Forever
I would have loved you
But
You took that choice away from me

-you can never force someone to stay

You left me with nothing
But
The memories of you
Drowning out the silence of you not here anymore

emma clark

You only knew what you lost
When you tried to replace me

One by one
Piece by piece
You wrecked me
Until I couldn't even recognize myself anymore

emma clark

You push I pull
You sit I stand
We are just two different people
Who happen to want two different things

We almost escaped the inevitable
We almost made it out alive
We almost created an everlasting love story

Almost
It's the word that gets you every damn time

emma clark

A delicate and tender daisy
Watered without warning
Picked before it could grow
Held to the muddy, cold ground
Forced to move a way a flower shouldn't
The flower was her
12 and delicate

During the time, she was searching for a sign of hope
A distraction of some sort
To her left, a white daisy with a bright yellow center stared back
like it had known her entire life.

She felt some sort of calm…
That's why a single daisy is her favorite flower.

Hands on her body that shouldn't be there
Cold brown dirty sticks in her hair
The smell of musk men surrounded her
They spread her legs like they wanted to taste
Every
Sweet
Drop

-She was only 12

emma clark

I craved the happy ever after
I longed for an endless love
It wasn't long until I realized I hung onto you
Only because..
I hoped you could've been the person for me
That I was for you

It was me who didn't love you enough
It was me who focused on the bad
Because in some part of me I..
Expected to be hurt the way I was used to

Not letting you in was my fault
Hurting you was his

She sat in her two story all brick home
Staring out of her four paneled window
She remembered her "first times"..

Her first times were created by bloody stained clothes
And the void of a painful piercing voice that spoke
"You will never be good enough".

I loved the hardest
You didn't love enough
Yet, here I am writing another sad poem about you
Because in some way despite everything
I
Still
Love
You

emma clark

I wish we could have been meant to be

You walked away
But you said

F o r e v e r

-Read between the lines

She craved love
He wanted lust
They hoped for two different things
Until he decided it wasn't good enough for him

Anymore

emma clark

SPRING

emma clark

Petal by petal
Stem by stem
I'm falling

Again

You planted in me for the first time
You engulfed me like I was a seed that needed watering
I collapsed into you; wilted and tender
You made me bloom
You became my greenhouse

emma clark

Counting Seconds

Whenever you're around
Everything I've always dreamed of feeling becomes real
You're everything I've ever wanted
I wanted the possibility of us because
It's all I have wanted since the second I met you

Everyone dreams of a forever love
Something I didn't know was possible until I met you
It's kind of like
finally taking off the training wheels
And
Before you know it..
You're in love
You didn't plan to fall in love..
It just happened
Without warning; all at once
Love
Until i was utterly consumed by the presence of someone

emma clark

Home isn't always a place
Home is you

A Theory

Maybe we're all meant for someone
Star crossed lovers of some kind
I didn't mean to meet you this early
But, I guess life had us next in line

HERO

You have the arms that make all of the superhero's look irrelevant
The arms I want to be wrapped in until the end of time
You have the baby blue eyes that seem so deep
the ocean can't even compare
You have the smile with dimples that could be moon craters
I choose you

You are my hero
Thank you for saving me

You were the first guy to call me beautiful
and I could see the love in your eyes.

That's something I had never felt before

Water the soil of self care
Plant the seed of loving again
Grow the life you have always longed for
One day
You will take a step back and see a beautiful garden
Created by nothing or no one except you
- the art in loving yourself again

Sticks and stones can't break your bones but words
will forever be the death of me.
-I was only fourteen

You can't live your life afraid of what other
people think of you.
You will never be able to grow.

I started writing to let out all of my emotions
But
When I write about you, it's like the break up happened
all over again
just in a different font.

What hurt the most wasn't what you did
I always knew you were capable of putting your selfishness first
It was the aftermath of it all
Nothing came out of it, you just hurt me because you could.
I will NEVER give anyone that power again.
-Friends can break your heart just as worse

emma clark

During the day I live without the images of you
At night it all hits me, of how it could've been different

How is it that me still wearing your shirt to sleep gives me comfort?
-It fills the void in my bed

I will forever dream
of the way you love
me

emma clark

I felt this brief feeling of wholeness
It was the spring season where the flowers
blossomed and it rained everyday
I saw you from across the street
You noticed no one but everyone noticed you
It was then that I realized you were mine and
that was the best feeling in the world

emma clark

Your lips welcomed me
Your eyes pulled me in
Before I could even think
We were intertwined in anyway possible
You suddenly and all at once became someone
I could never forget

My first love was innocent, it was the kind
that just felt young and dumb.
Making mistakes and forgiving because we didn't
even really know right from wrong.

My second love..
That was real.
It was being engulfed all together
It was also.. if not the worst heartbreak of all time

Hoping to just wake up and it all be a dream
I wanted to see you downstairs on christmas morning
helping open all of the gifts.
Seeing your stocking on the fireplace. I wanted you to
just be there, but the sick and twisted reality was I knew
you were never coming back to our home

-My dad left when I was fourteen

emma clark

I wonder how you can look into the eyes of someone
you have created a life with for two decades
and just decide to give up
-divorce affects the kids more

If he loved you he would've stayed
Don't spend all of your time waiting
it simply won't happen
if it was never real to begin with

-Accepting

emma clark

 I told you I loved you because I felt every single ounce of it
You only said it because you knew it was the only way
you could get my clothes to fall off

-I wasn't being easy, I was being gullible

It was never the arguing

It was the silence

because we simply had nothing else to say.

Why did you love him?

Because he was like a cloudless sky.
His voice painted pictures of our future in my mind.
His radiant blue eyes spoke without him saying anything.
His energy was as burning as the sun.
He gave me so many reasons to stay, and so many more
to keep fighting.
I loved him fearlessly.
He was the reason I fell in love with sunsets.

emma clark

SUMMER

As we laid and looked up at the stars
I imagined a life with you
Your head in my lap as my favorite song played
We just lied there without moving

And even though you weren't meant for me…
In that moment
I would've done anything for time to stop

emma clark

Brown eyes and stars will always make me think of you

emma clark

My love for you was like the ocean
Depths of colors, and the unknown
You discovered the parts of me no one else had

11 A.M.
Warm and sunny rays bounced off her skin
The salty blue water ran off of his
She looked up and all she could see was the silhouette of the most
beautiful human that she had ever seen

4 P.M.
Pink cotton candy skies rolled in
Captivating every moment
She felt it all at once

8 P.M.
The moon glided into the sky
She looked into his eyes knowing everything he felt
He grabbed her face and told her
She was everything he ever wanted

You said I had eyes for someone else
But
You were the only one who could see

Me.

Not only do I crave to be alive
But I crave to live
I want to seek the beauty in life
Find a person that consumes it
Travel to the deepest parts of the world
Dance in the moment without fear
Cry from laughter
I just simply long for *joy*

-anything is possible if you just try

emma clark

You are only going to be happy
when you're happy within yourself first

-go back to the beginning of you

She stares right back at me
She is beautiful
She is kind
She is worthy
She is a long and growing list of everything she was designed to be

It wasn't until she loved herself that she could really see

Mirrors are only the representation of how we view ourselves

-loving yourself

It may not be easy all of the time
Sometimes you may feel like giving up and forgetting

What kind of life would you be living if all you ever did was stop?
Life is
Beautiful
And
Messy
However, life is always worth living

-keep going it gets better

It has always been my passion
It has given me the power to be anywhere I wanted to be in the world
Regardless of the hard times, and all of my struggles
I have found the real heart of the world
I have found the love that never dies
It has a name
No. 2 pencil and my worn, fourteen year old diary

Anyone who has ever known me can always say this.
The "you" in I love you is important.
It isn't like they are just naming anything they love
It's specific
They are reminding you that they choose **you**
Never forget that

And if in some crazy twisted time, we find our way back to each other.
We would just have defied all odds

-I like our chances

No matter where, and no matter what
We weren't just an accident

-A firm believer that everything happens for a reason

There will be times when people leave
when love just dies.
The world is going down the longest spiral
but time still passes, new people show up and the sun still sets.
I've learned to see the world for what people offer
and the things I want in return.
There is a reason it takes time. You must heal.
Let your hurt soak it all up because one day,
you won't be the same person you were.
Then, waiting for everything at the right time will have been
worth it.

emma clark

His dimples
His hugs
His heart
Our love
But nothing good lasts forever
Right?

emma clark

You are the pleasant gardener that made my soul grow
-always count your blessings

Our **crazy** love story was always **beautiful**
-He will know

Regardless where you are in the world
the golden sun captivates,
almost swallowing anyone into oblivion.
It is the most peaceful moment in time where nothing else matters.
You can feel the blissful moment of love
-when I realized I loved nothing more than sunsets

I will never apologize for loving you but I am sorry to myself
for trying to make you love me

-You can't force someone to want you

If you were to call I couldn't promise myself that I wouldn't answer
-I think I still love you

She longed for a love like her parents
Until it ended in a disastrous story
Then she realized it was already too late to take it back.
-They started it but he ended it

He walked to the edge where the sand met the water
She watched as he looked at everything around him
all she could think was that she wasn't good enough
or he was searching for a distraction.
He walked back up to her, and handed her
the most beautiful shell she had ever seen.
It was then she realized it wasn't him that she couldn't trust,
It was her.

emma clark

Our story portrayed the most telling story.
Even if it didn't last, and no one knew.
You and I will always know the way it was.
It is one that can't be forgotten.

-I didn't want you to be a secret

You make me love the way
no one
has before.
-Not my first love but someone I'll never forget

Just know that you go through all of these questions to get to the answer
You continue down a path
Until it finally hits you that you deserve better.
If it wasn't for the feeling, hurting, and breaking
You wouldn't know how to love. You wouldn't know how to take care
of someone's heart just like your own. Sometimes you have to stop
being a guardian to your soul.
Let it all out, and just live with no regrets for the future.

-finally taking my own advice

You created a sense of art in my eyes.
It was almost like painting a picture because
the more invested I became in you the more
it just all made sense.
I loved you, more than I loved myself.

And that was the problem.

-Never give all of yourself away

emma clark

I wish we could have met at different circumstances
-3 A.M. wanderless thoughts

Your eyes always told the deepest story
-sight first at love

SUMMER SKIES

Your eyes are just like the sunny sky at 1 p.m.
Crystal and blue
Your heart is just like the sun at 5 p.m.
Yellow and gold
Your mind is just like mine at 12 a.m.
Wandering in thoughts
Of what it would be like
If we had never given us a shot

emma clark

FALL

His eyes resembled the sweetest chocolate
He had a familiar scent
His mind danced around hers in the moment
The sky glistened with hope
Hope of a new beginning

But who knew that even the sweetest chocolate could turn bitter
Without even taking a bite

emma clark

You were the person who always broke my heart
But the only one who knew how to put it back together

emma clark

After we spoke about our love being timeless

The clock ran out of time

emma clark

No matter what the circumstances were
It would have always been you

It was then when I realized,
You were only supposed to come into my life to pull me away from the
Somber shadows of the night.
Remember darling,
Sometimes people are only supposed to be your sunrise

-the girl who never settles for a sunset

Her eye dimples are awkward
Her hips are too wide
She doesn't have a thigh gap
Her voice gets too squeaky

Are you sure he likes her?

She wanted to scream in her face
But
Her reflection couldn't speak back
-when I didn't love myself

emma clark

Your real prince charming will buy you flowers without hesitation

Watching the romance movies, and reading the
novels it all became a stereotype..
You see the love that people die for

I want the kind you live for.

-the girl who will always be a hopeless romantic

The room light flickering
The white lit moon gazing into the kitchen window
The cold dark tile floor rested underneath her feet
The peaceful quiet music playing in the background

His hand in hers
Hers in his
His other around her waist
Hers on his shoulder
They danced
And she realized she had everything she ever wanted
He leans in to kiss her and before he spoke

She woke up

-dancing in the kitchen will always be a dream of mine

How could it ever be the right person at the wrong time?

If two souls are destined to be together
Don't you know that they would have both stayed?

-the pain swallowing truth

emma clark

Every sun I ever watched set
Every cloud I ever saw
Every star I ever wished upon

It was always you

But

It was never me
Right?

I talked to the universe about you
I spoke about the time I saw you for the very first time
The way you made my heart practically skip beats
The way you laughed and joked with me
The way you told me you were going to *freak out*
because you are way too ticklish

I spoke about all of the things that happened in those short few months
Even if you didn't know it I was crazy about you
But you decided you wanted her instead

 Damn you, universe

emma clark

I lay by my phone
Hoping to see it light up the dark cold room with your name
I have done this every night since you left
Questioning why I wasn't the one for you or you being the one for me
It wasn't until the last time I saw you that made me understand
that at the end of the day,
when the sun sets in our Alabama skies you'll never need me.
No matter how much I need you.

Here's to the boys who daydream
The ones that sacrifice everything for her
You are the kind that made me believe in love

Father

I spent years questioning why you chose a new life with someone
Why you fought for a new beginning when your
"old" chapter wasn't even finished being written

I guess some things I will never understand

-the fourteen year old me

Sometimes it's okay to walk away
It's okay to not win every argument

I couldn't even try with you because in most cases
you'd break my heart when I was just trying to fix yours.

-The mom that was just left broken too

emma clark

We were only ever going to be parallel lines
And worlds that never could collide

-I wish I would have known

emma clark

They say to write what you feel

How am I supposed to do that when all I am staring at is
The blank spaces between my thoughts that can't even be seen?
-Before I knew poetry

BLUE MOON

I used to question if you missed me
Maybe if it was just a thought so brief
You didn't have to sit in sorrow
But I wanted you to feel hollow
I wanted you to see how it felt
When I was left and needed help
Perhaps if it would've worked out
I wouldn't be missing you right now
But it's only that ever blue moon
When I happen to think of you

I will always be the girl who smiles at sunsets, books,
and every Nicholas Sparks movie made.

-I will always unapologetically be Emma Clark